KOMBUCHA MANUAL

TREATMENTS AND HEALTH BENEIFITS OF KOMBUCHA

DR. MARC PARSONS

Table of Contents

CHAPTER ONE

KOMBUCHA

Kombucha's health benefits are what?

Sweet and fizzy, kombucha is a fermented tea drink. Do the health benefits of this popular beverage outweigh the risks?

Probiotic bacteria are found in kombucha. Health-enhancing microorganisms can be found in these foods.

As a result, some research suggests that kombucha may have health benefits for the gut, the brain, the immune system, and the liver. According to these findings, more research is needed to confirm these advantages.

What exactly is kombucha?

Kombucha is a tea-based beverage that is sweet and fizzy due to the addition of sugar, tea, and bacteria. Yellow-orange in color, it has a mildly sour flavor.

Sweetened green or black tea can be fermented with a symbiotic colony of bacteria and yeast to produce kombucha (SCOBY). The SCOBY's yeast breaks down the sugar in the tea and releases friendly probiotic bacteria during the fermentation process.

After fermentation, kombucha becomes carbonated, which is why the beverage is fizzy.

Tea is used to make kombucha, a fizzy, sweet-and-sour beverage. Hair loss to cancer and AIDS are just some of the ailments it is said to help alleviate or prevent. Some of the drink's components may be beneficial to your health, but there is little scientific evidence to support these claims.

It's hard to believe that kombucha has been around for so long. Japan and Russia were early adopters after the Chinese. In Europe, it became popular in the early 20th century. As a health and energy drink, it's gaining popularity in the United States.

Kombucha's Potential Health Benefits

However, preliminary studies show that it may improve your digestive system and more. Listed below are some of the potential advantages that scientists are still investigating.

Boosting Metabolism may be beneficial in some cases.

In order to lose weight, you'll probably look into anything that can rev up your metabolism.

I don't believe that kombucha is a magic potion for weight loss. However, some types of kombucha's green tea contains the antioxidant epigallocatechin-3-gallate (EGCG), which may be the key to a slightly faster metabolism.

Green tea contains a catechin compound called EGCG.

Researchers from the Journal of Nutritional Biochemistry found that catechins can increase metabolic rates in adults. There are only a few small studies on the topic, and the authors of this review note that more research is needed to determine the true metabolic effects of EGCG.

Constipation may benefit from this.

Some claim that kombucha can help balance gut bacteria and alleviate gastrointestinal problems because of its probiotic content, but more research, according to the Cleveland Clinic, is needed to confirm this.

A "prominent lactobacillus population" was found in kombucha, according to a study published in Food Microbiology in April 2014. Lactobacillus is a common type of probiotic, so it's possible that kombucha could help stabilize the digestive tract and prevent infections and inflammation.. Drinking kombucha may help alleviate irritable bowel syndrome, inflammatory bowel disease, bloating, and constipation if that's what's going on.

Possible De-inflammatory Effects

According to a June 2019 article in chronic inflammation is linked to a wide range of health conditions, including heart disease, diabetes, arthritis, allergies, and respiratory illnesses like COPD.

CHAPTER TWO

Although it isn't a first-line treatment for any chronic disease, kombucha may be a helpful addition to a healthy diet, active lifestyle, and prescription medication. This is because the teas used to brew kombucha contain antioxidant polyphenols, which have been shown to reduce inflammation in the body.

According to a review published in Microbial Ecology in Health and Disease in February 2015, eating gut-friendly foods may help lower inflammation in the intestines, and kombucha in particular may be helpful.

Chronic low-grade inflammation is thought to be a factor in IBS and other inflammatory bowel diseases, as well as other gastro-intestinal disorders. Gut dysbiosis, or an imbalance of good and bad bacteria in the gut, may be to blame for this inflammation. According to the Microbial Ecology in Health and Disease review, an immune system response is triggered when bad bacteria outnumber good bacteria, and it is this response that causes inflammation.

Helps to Prevent Cancer in Some People

Further research is needed to determine whether kombucha can help prevent certain types of cancer. An article published in the Journal of Nutritional Biochemistry notes that kombucha has antioxidant properties that help the body rid itself of free radicals and other harmful substances that promote the growth of cancerous cells.

According to the National Cancer Institute, kombucha inhibits angiogenesis, the growth of new blood vessels, according to a study published in the journal Biomedicine & Preventive Nutrition in January-February 2013. (8,9) Angiogenesis, or the growth of new blood vessels, is critical to the growth of prostate cancer tumors, according to a new study. Researchers concluded that kombucha could reduce the survival of prostate cancer cells by inhibiting angiogenesis. Further investigation is, of course, required.

Gluconic acid, glucuronic acid, lactase, polyphenols, and vitamin C are some of the compounds in kombucha that may inhibit cancer growth, according to the review in the Journal of Nutritional Biochemistry.

Strengthening the Immune System may also be beneficial.

There may also be an immune system benefit to the gut-healthy properties of kombucha.

According to John Hopkins Medicine, the lining of the intestines produces antibodies that aid in the body's defenses. This is an important point to keep in mind. About 70% of the body's immune system can be found in the gut, according to a study.

Thus, according to Zenhausern, a strong immune system is dependent on a healthy gut. According to Zenhausern, kombucha's fermenting bacteria can boost immunity because of the good bacteria they provide.

6. Helps in the Treatment of Depression

Some of the most common symptoms of depression are a

sense of sadness and hopelessness.

There is no evidence that kombucha is linked to depression in any way. Some studies suggest that changes in the microbiome (the bacterial environment of the gut) may be associated with mental health issues, such as depression and anxiety, and a February 2017 review published in the Annals of General Psychiatry suggests as much.

It is important to note that 95 percent of serotonin is produced in the gut, not the brain, and thus optimal gut health is critical to mental health and mood regulation. When it comes to improving mood and battling depression, "this is why it is always important to address gut health," she says.

Helps Maintain a Healthy Cardiovascular System

Cardiovascular disease increases your chances of having a stroke or heart attack, but you can improve your cardiovascular health by making healthy lifestyle changes, according to the Centers for Disease Control (CDC).

In order to stay healthy, you should eat a diet rich in fruits, vegetables, whole grains, and lean protein. Exercise, medication, and yes, kombucha, should all be part of your regimen.

Research published in the Journal of Chemistry suggests

that kombucha may have a positive effect on cholesterol levels. Among other things, the CDC cites high cholesterol as a risk factor for heart disease.

Kombucha's cholesterol-lowering properties have yet to be proven in human trials.

However, a study published in the journal Pharmaceutical Biology in April 2015 found that rats given kombucha had lower levels of LDL (bad) cholesterol and higher levels of HDL (good) cholesterol. Kombucha may also improve cholesterol levels in humans, but further research is needed. I don't know yet.

8. May Improve Liver Function.

Kombucha, on the other hand, has the potential to detoxify the body, which could improve liver health. According to the Journal of Chemistry, regular consumption of the beverage may reduce the amount of work your liver has to do over time.

CHAPTER THREE

Additionally, rats given kombucha showed decreased levels of thiobarbituric acid reactive substances in their livers in the Pharmaceutical Biology study. Cell and tissue damage can be measured by the presence of this organic compound. Clinical trials are still needed to determine if the benefits of the treatment are long-lasting.

Plays a role in reducing blood sugar levels

Diabetes and insulin resistance may also benefit from kombucha consumption. According to a study, the tea can lower postprandial (after-meal) glucose levels by inhibiting a pancreatic protein called – amylase.

After 30 days of drinking kombucha, rats with diabetes were cured and their liver and kidney function improved, according to a study in Pharmaceutical Biology.

It's possible that kombucha could one day be used as an alternative treatment for diabetes in addition to traditional methods such as weight loss, diet and exercise, oral medications as well as insulin.

Assist in Retaining a Healthy Body Mass Index

If you like soda or juice but want something with fewer calories and sugar to help you lose or maintain your weight, consider kombucha as an option.

Sugar contains a lot of empty calories, so if you eat too much of it, you run the risk of gaining weight.

Keep in mind that kombucha does contain sugar (most of the sugar is fermented, but some remains in the final product). Even so, according to Boston-based RDN Rebecca Stib, co-founder of Nutritious Gifts, a typical drink may only contain 6 to 8 grams of sugar per serving.

In the case of two-serving bottles, "you'll have to double the amount," warns Stib, "but it's still lower than your typical serving of a can of soda or juice drink, which can be up to 25 g per serving."

In 8 ounces of GTS kombucha, there are 30 calories and 8 grams of sugar, according to the company's website. In contrast, the Coca-Cola website estimates that an 8-ounce can of soda contains 60 calories and 16 grams of sugar.

Digestive health

A little bit of investigation.

Kombucha and other fermented foods, according to Trusted Source, have a high concentration of probiotics. When it comes to probiotics, they're just like the good bacteria in your digestive system.

CHAPTER FOUR

Probiotics in the diet may help improve gut health in general. It's possible that probiotics help the body's microbial ecosystem stay in good shape.

Some evidence suggests that probiotics may be beneficial in the following areas, according to the National Center for Complementary and Integrative HealthTrusted Source:

• Antibiotic-induced diarrhea

Chronic inflammation of the gastrointestinal tract

IBS (chronic constipation syndrome)

While foods and beverages containing probiotics may have some health benefits, the majority of these benefits are derived from probiotic supplements.

The link between kombucha and gut health needs further

investigation, but the association suggests that it may aid digestion.

Immune system function is strongly linked to gut health. Immune health may be improved by maintaining a healthy balance of gut bacteria, according to research.

Probiotic-rich foods and beverages may improve gut health if consumed in moderation.

Risk of infection

In the fermentation process of kombucha, a substance called acetic acid is produced, which is also found in vinegar. Acetic acid has been shown to have antimicrobial properties, according to research.

It's possible, based on other research, that kombucha has antimicrobial properties, making it a useful weapon in the fight against a variety of bacteria.

Antibiotics may prevent infections by killing the bacteria that cause them before they are absorbed into the body, according to this research.

Human studies, on the other hand, have not confirmed this effect.

The state of one's mind

Drinking kombucha enriched with probiotics may improve mental health. A possible link between probiotics and depression has been suggested by some sources.

Anti-inflammatory properties of kombucha have been linked to a reduction in the severity of depressive symptoms.

A look back at the year 2017

According to Trusted Source, there is strong evidence that probiotic supplements can help alleviate the symptoms of depression. But further research is needed to prove their effectiveness for this purpose.

Nevertheless, despite the fact that some studies

Probiotic-rich foods and beverages, such as kombucha, are thought to have a positive effect on mental health, but there have been no studies to support this claim.

Inflammation of the heart

Cholesterol levels that are too high can raise the risk of heart disease.

In rats, a 2015 study found that kombucha helped lower cholesterol levels linked to heart disease, and other studies support this finding.

Probiotic supplements may help lower cardiovascular disease risk, according to Trusted Source.

It is important to keep in mind that results in rats don't always translate to human outcomes. Kombucha's ability to lower the risk of heart disease in humans has yet to be proven.

There are a number of factors that can affect cholesterol levels and heart disease risk.

Hepatic wellness

To protect cells from damage caused by molecules, Kombucha contains antioxidants.

Some studies, including a 2014Trusted Source study, suggest that kombucha consumption may protect against drug-induced liver damage in animals.

This raises the possibility that kombucha can help maintain healthy liver function by decreasing liver inflammation.

In contrast, there is currently no scientific evidence that drinking kombucha improves human liver health.

The treatment of type 2 diabetes

There is some evidence that kombucha can help manage type 2 diabetes in animal studies, but the results are inconclusive.

According to a study conducted in 2012, kombucha helped diabetic rats control their blood sugar levels.

The fact remains that kombucha has not been proven to lower blood sugar levels in humans.

The added sugar in most kombucha drinks can raise blood sugar levels. Drinking kombucha, a sugary beverage, can have a negative impact on blood sugar control in diabetics.

CHAPTER FIVE

Ingredients for Kombucha

Yeast, sugar, and black tea are the three primary ingredients in kombucha. For a week or more, the mixture is left to rest. There is a small amount of alcohol and bacteria in the drink during this time. If you've ever had kimchi, sauerkraut, or yogurt made from dairy, you'll recognize the term "fermentation."

A SCOBY is a layer of bacteria and acids that forms on top of the liquid (symbiotic colony of bacteria and yeast). A SCOBY can be used to increase the amount of kombucha you make.

Bacteria found in kombucha, such as lactic acid bacteria, can be used as a probiotic. B vitamins are abundant in kombucha as well.

Home kombucha-making instructions

People can make their own SCOBY at home by heating up and combining water, sugar, black or green tea, and premade kombucha in a brew kettle.

Let the SCOBY sit in sweetened tea for a week or more at room temperature. Allow the SCOBY to breathe by attaching a cloth to the top of the jar with elastic.

Depending on personal preference, kombucha can be ready to drink in 6–12 days. The longer it sits, the less sweet it becomes.

The best place to buy Kombucha is at the supermarket

A wide variety of kombucha brands are available for purchase online, including pre-made kombucha and the ingredients needed to make kombucha yourself.

- kombucha

- SCOBY

kit for brewing kombucha at home

Risks

When making kombucha at home, it's important to keep an eye on it because it can ferment too long. Kombucha can also be contaminated if it is not made in a sterile environment by a person.

Making kombucha at home is risky because of the possibility

of contamination or overfermentation.

Sugar is a common ingredient in most kombuchas. Drinking sugar-sweetened beverages on a regular basis can have a negative impact on your health in a number of ways.

If you drink a lot of sugary drinks like soda, you'll gain weight and raise your blood sugar levels.

Kombucha brands with less than 4 grams (1 teaspoon) of added sugar per serving may be the best bet when looking for kombucha.

Summary

Drinking Kombucha may have numerous health advantages. Research is ongoing, however, and not all benefits have been demonstrated in studies involving human subjects.

Even though kombucha has been linked to cancer prevention and weight loss, there is currently insufficient evidence to support these claims.

It's safe to drink kombucha as part of a healthy diet if it's made correctly or purchased from the store.

THE END